The Complete Anthology of Lute Music from Musick's Monument By Thomas Mace

The complete anthology of lute music from the 1676 London Edition

Transcribed & Edited for Classical Guitar by Andrew Shepard-Smith

1 2 3 4 5 6 7 8 9 0

Visit us on the Web at www.melbay.com — E-mail us at email@melbay.com

Contents

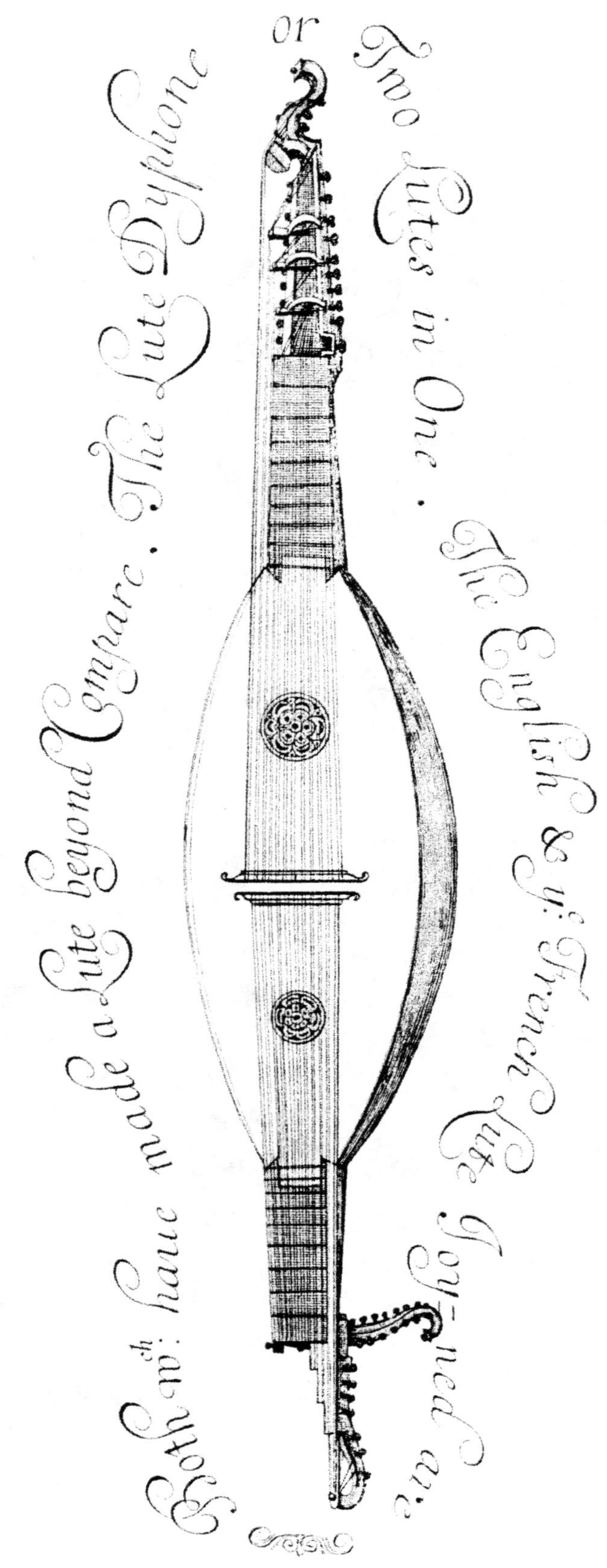

From Thomas Mace, *Musick's Monument,* facsimile reprint. *Monuments of Music and Music Literature in Facsimile, Second Series, XVII* (New York: Broude Brothers Limited, 1966). Reproduced by arrangement with Broude Brothers Limited.

From Thomas Mace, *Musick's Monument,* facsimile reprint. *Monuments of Music and Music Literature in Facsimile, Second Series, XVII* (New York: Broude Brothers Limited, 1966). Reproduced by arrangement with Broude Brothers Limited.

From Thomas Mace, *Musick's Monument,* facsimile reprint. Monuments of *Music and Music Literature in Facsimile, Second Series, XVII* (New York: Broude Brothers Limited, 1966). Reproduced by arrangement with Broude Brothers Limited.

Foreword

Original Titles

Titles and section headings in this edition do not appear exactly as they did in the original London edition of *Musick's Monument*. For example, Mace did not classify or title "The First and Second Sets of Præludes," as these were assigned in order to group the contents of this anthology. And although the works contained within each suite are placed in the order in which Mace wrote, he typically referred to them as "setts," and through terminology such as *"The First Sett of Lessons,"* however, he does occasionally refer to them as "suits."

Photographic Reproductions

The images that appear in this anthology were taken from the 1966 facsimile reprint of *Musick's Monument* published by Broude Brothers, Ltd., and were reproduced by arrangement with Broude Brothers, Ltd. 2001.

Transcription Notes

The specific lute tuning for both sets of preludes and the first four suites (in their original keys) are referred to by Mace as the *flat-tuning:* g′, e′, c′, a, e, B, A, G, F, E, D, C. He indicates a small change of tuning for the next two suites to: g′, e′, c′, a, e, B, A, G, F♯, E, D, C. The seventh suite requires a change to: g′, e′, c′, a, e, B, A, G, F, E, D, B′, while the eighth suite is set in what Mace refers to as the *new-tuning:* g′, e′, b′, g, e, B, A, G, F♯, E, D, B′. *Nightengal* is also set in the flat-tuning, however the final work, the lengthy *Voluntary,* was written to be performed on the theorboe with a re-entrant tuning. Mace's original tuning was: g, d′, a′, f, c, G, F, E, D, C, B′, A′, G′, although the work is presented here in the key of A minor.

Occasional added pitches are referenced in the score with brackets, and notes in parentheses indicate pitches that, while in the original tablature, may not be playable on the modern guitar or can be inserted at the discretion of the performer. To further make this anthology playable, octave transpositions in the bass voice were necessary. These are referenced in the score by the sign (8), placed below the note, to indicate where the note was raised an octave, and (16), where the note has been raised two. All notes lowered one octave use the same indication, placed above the note. And since lute tablature can be ambiguous as to the precise duration of pitches, durations are based upon musical and idiomatic factors.

Mace indicated left and right-hand fingerings in some of his tablatures, however, those are only present in this edition when referenced. And while the original time signatures were retained, unless otherwise noted, all repeat signs are editorial. For greater score clarity, first and second endings are not used.

Acknowledgments

I would like to thank Paul Reilly for the inspiration to take on this project, and my wife, Vanessa, for her unending love and support while I completed it. I also wish to express my thanks to Clare Callahan, Richard White, Michael Howell, Richard Yates, and Stanley Yates for their invaluable assistance in proofing.

Ornaments

Ornaments (or "graces") in these transcriptions have been preserved in their original appearance and placement according to the original lute tablature. Modern scholars and performers should insert the appropriate ornaments in response to Mace's directions, at the signs which are presented in the transcriptions. A Table of Ornaments, which represents Mace's written instructions, has been illustrated on the following page (however, no such table is present in the original). Mace wrote out only a few of the fifteen main ornaments, and those durations have been preserved as in the original. The remaining ornaments are subject to interpretation, and plausible realizations are offered.

Table of Ornaments

The Shake

Mace gives no indication as to the note values or duration of ornaments.

The Beate

The Back-Fall

The Half-Fall

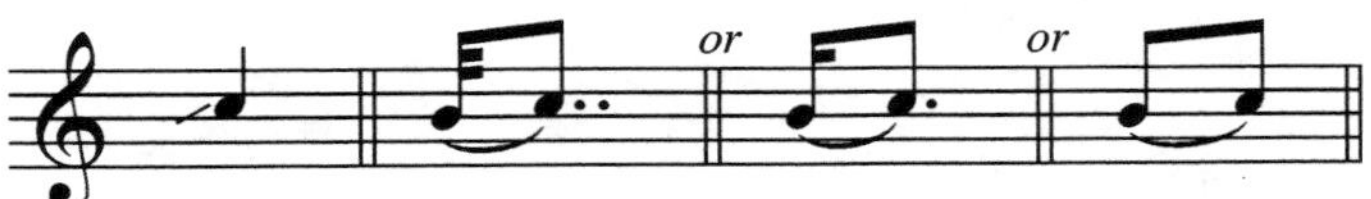

The Whole-Fall

or

The Spinger

Where the first note is loud and the second note is barely audible.

The Ascending Elevation

The Descending Elevation

Ascending Single Relish

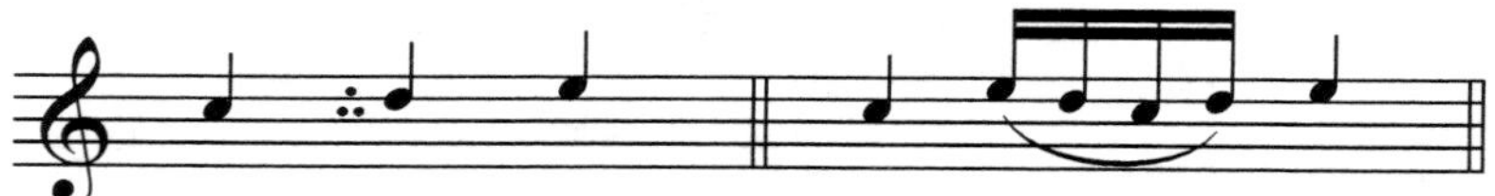

Descending Single Relish

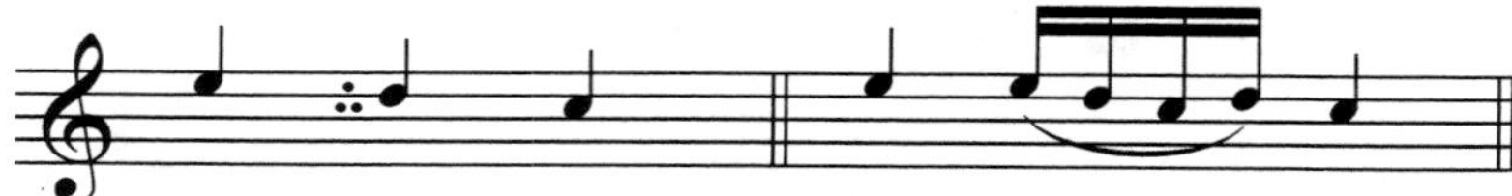

The Double Relish

Where every note is to be articulated.

The Slur

All slurs are *hammer-ons.*

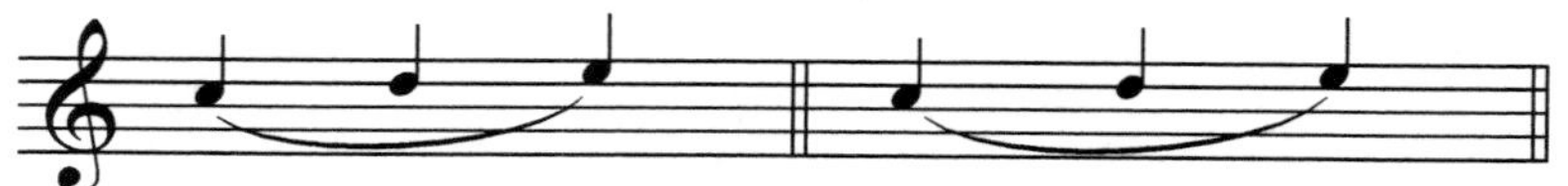

The Slide

All slides are *pull-offs.*

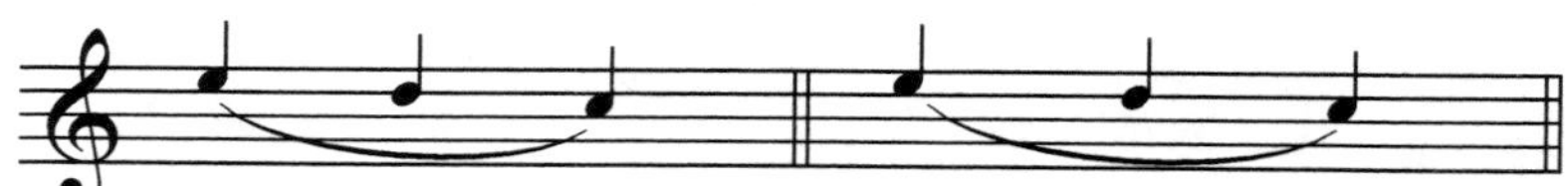

The Sting

Where the thumb is removed from the back of the neck and the string is pushed and pulled slightly from nut to bridge.

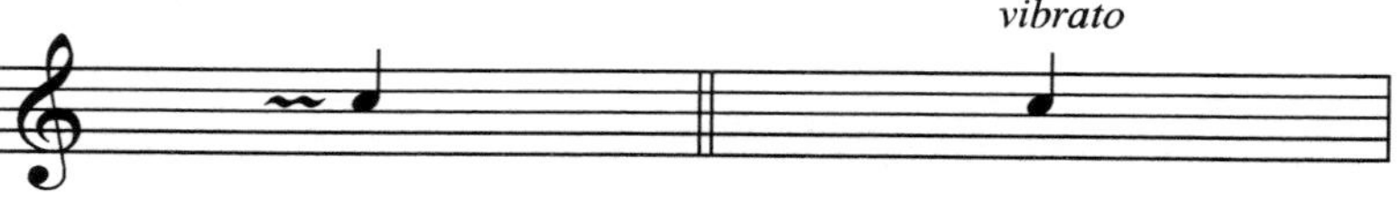

The Futt/Tut

Where the note is struck with one finger and then immediately and forcefully stopped with another.

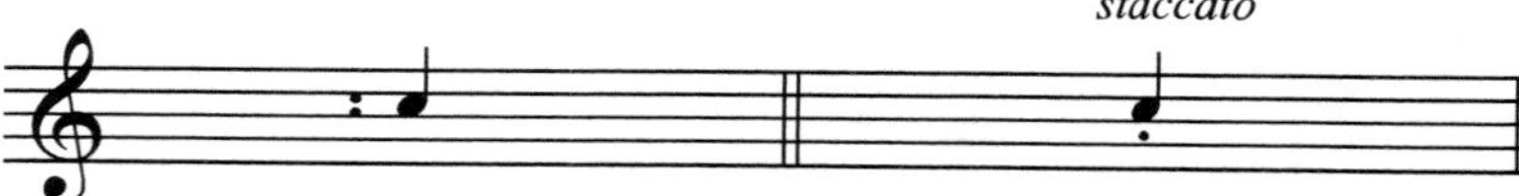

Soft and Loud Play

Mace gives no other dynamic consideration.

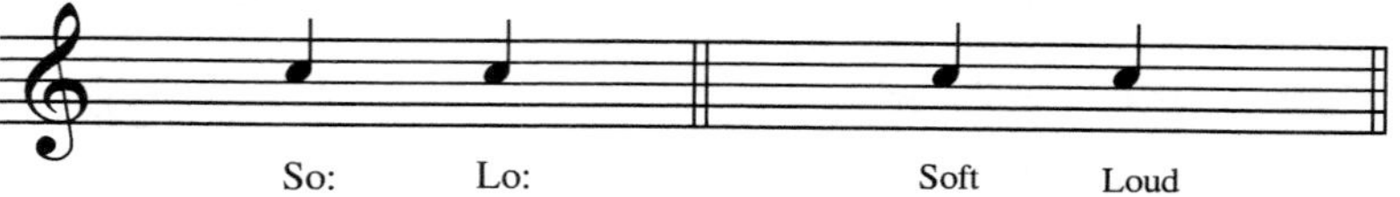

The Pause

Mace gives no indication of exact duration.

The First and Second Set of Præludes

(Derived from Chapter 14-24 of *Musick's Monument*)

The First Set of Præludes

Transcribed and Edited by
Andrew Shepard-Smith

Thomas Mace
(c. 1612 - c. 1706)

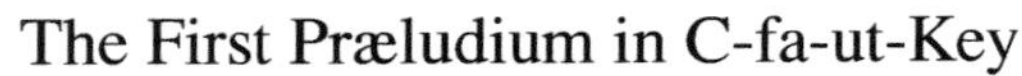

The First Præludium in C-fa-ut-Key

The Second Prælude in D-sol-re

The Third Prælude in E-la-mi
⑥=E
The Fourth Prælude in F-fa-ut
⑥=D
The Fifth Prælude in Gam-ut
⑥=E

The Sixth Prælude in A-re

(8)
VII5
V3

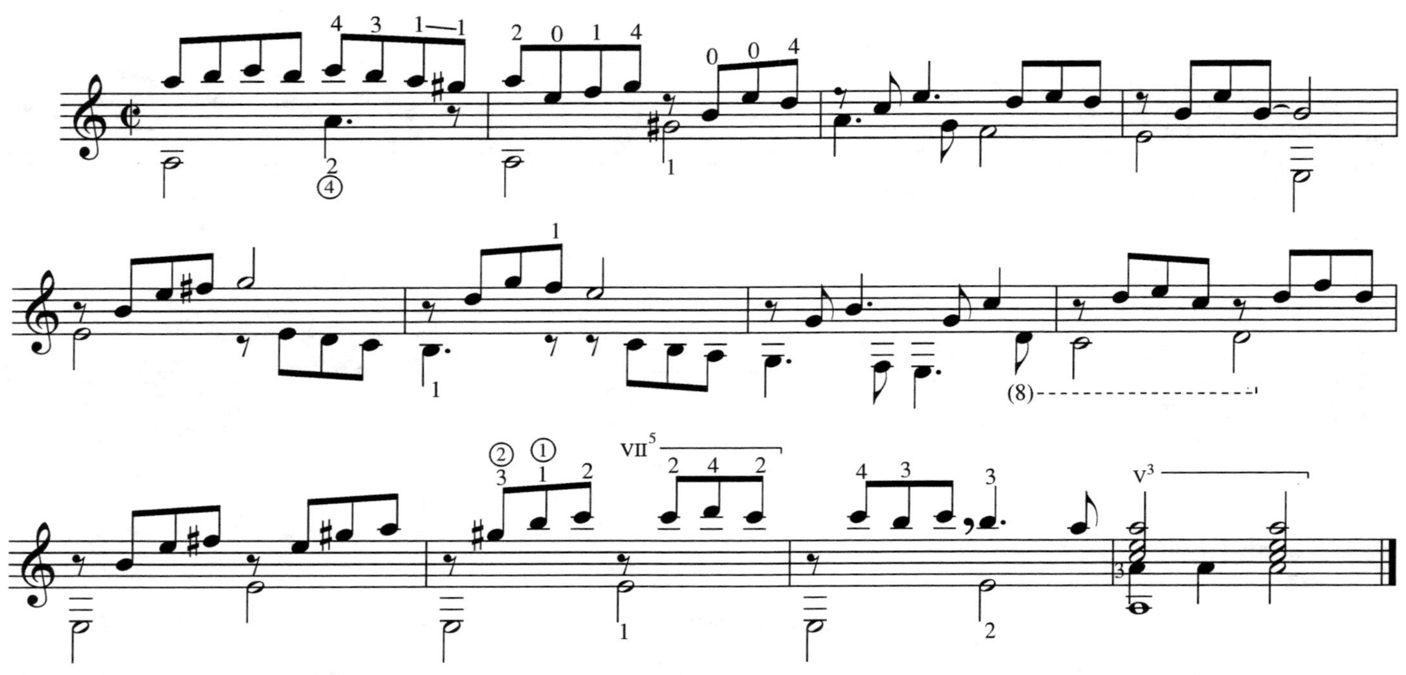

The Seventh Prælude for Fingering

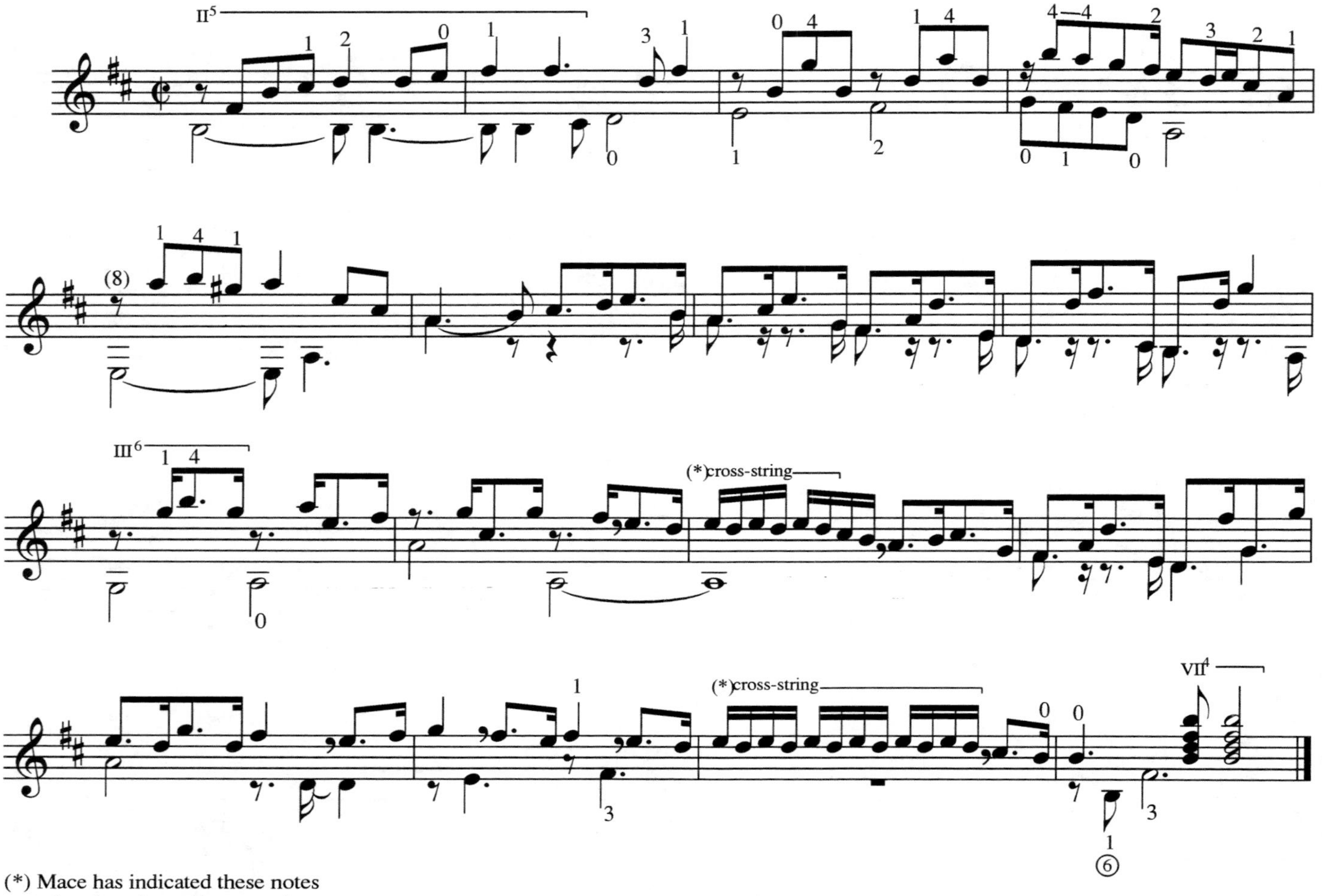
II5
(8)
III6
(*)cross-string
(*)cross-string
VII4

(*) Mace has indicated these notes to be played on adjacent strings.

The Second Set of Præludes

The First Prælude in C-fa-ut

The Second Prælude in the Tenth Above C-fa-ut

The Third Prælude in the Fifth Above C-fa-ut

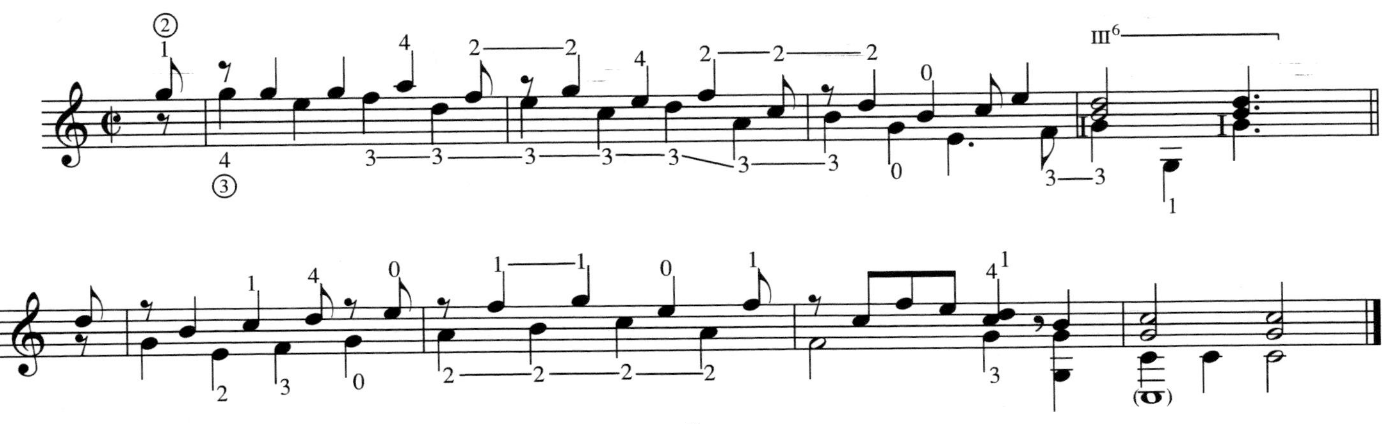

The Fourth Prælude in the Eighth Above C-fa-ut

The Eight Lute Suites

(Derived from Chapter 24-38 of *Musick's Monument*)

Suite No. 1

(original C major)

Transcribed and Edited by
Andrew Shepard-Smith

Thomas Mace
(c. 1612 - c. 1706)

Prælude

⑥= E

Mace's Mistress

The Off-Spring (or the Second Part to Mace's Mistress) *

(*) Mace writes that the "Off-Spring" can be played either in consort with Mace's Mistress, or as a solo. When performed as a duo, he indicates that the last two notes of the fourth measure, and the first three notes of the fifth measure may be left unplayed in this part as the notes are exactly the same as in "Mace's Mistress." He adds that, "although it will not introduce any discord, it is generally not accounted as being handsome to play the same thing upon several instruments."

Coranto I

(8) (8) (8)

II[4]

4④

II[4]

(8) (8) (8)

Coranto-*I Like My Humour Well*

I I I (8) (8) (8) 2 (8) (8) (8)

(8) (8) (8) (8) (8) 0 4 (8)

(8) (8) 2 4 1 2 1 2 2

4 (8)

Coranto II

Suite No. 2

(original F major)

Transcribed and Edited by
Andrew Shepard-Smith

Thomas Mace
(c. 1612 - c. 1706)

Prælude

Allmaine

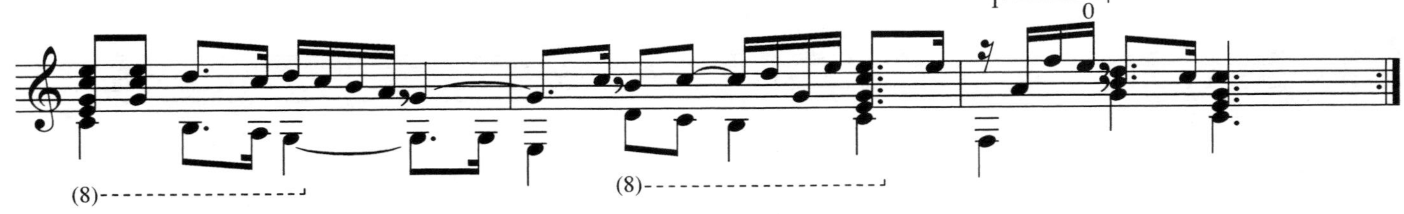

Ayre I

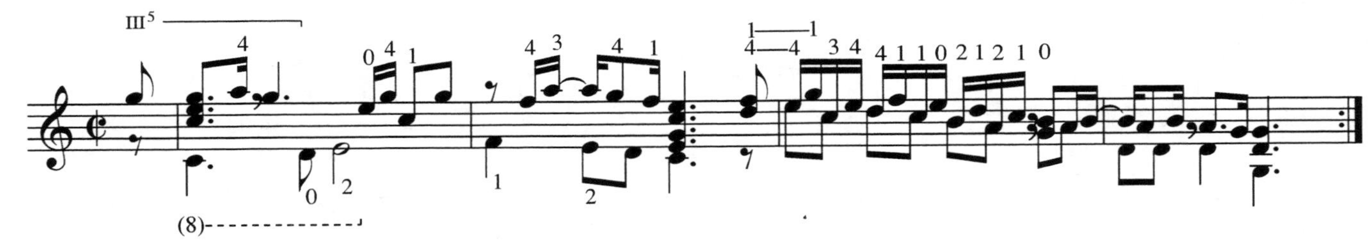

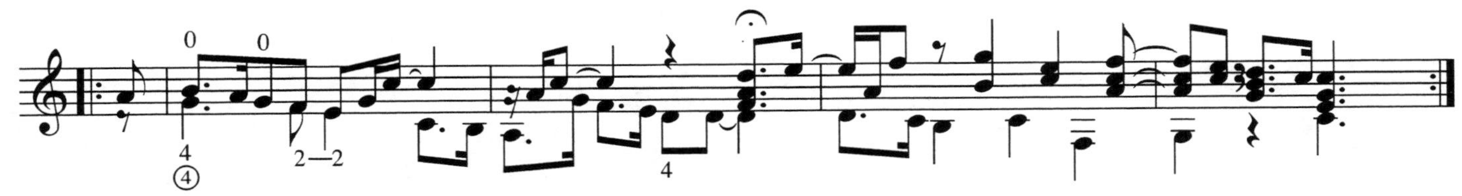

Ayre II

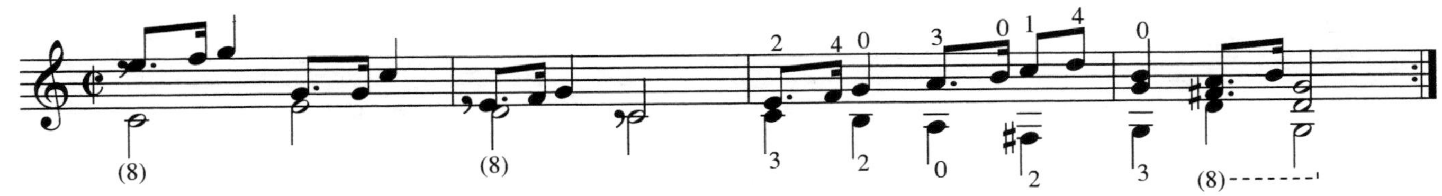

Coranto

Tattle de Moy

Suite No. 3

Transcribed and Edited by
Andrew Shepard-Smith

Thomas Mace
(c. 1612 - c. 1706)

Prælude

A florish or short come-off for the end of any lesson of the like. [Optional ending.]

Allmaine

Coranto

Galliard-Penitent
Lo:
So:
Hab-Nab
So:
Lo:
So:

[A Piece Without Title]

(*) Original time signature $\frac{6}{4}$

Suite No. 4

Transcribed and Edited by
Andrew Shepard-Smith

Thomas Mace
(c. 1612 - c. 1706)

Prælude

Allmaine

Galliard

Coranto I
So:
Lo:
So:
Coranto II

Seraband
So:
Lo:
So:
Tattle de Moy
So:
Lo:
So:
Lo:

Suite No. 5

Transcribed and Edited by
Andrew Shepard-Smith

Thomas Mace
(c. 1612 - c. 1706)

Prælude

Ayre

Coranto

Seraband
So:
Lo:
So:
Tattle de Moy
So:

Suite No. 6

Transcribed and Edited by
Andrew Shepard-Smith

Thomas Mace
(c. 1612 - c. 1706)

Prælude

Allmaine

Coranto

Galliard

Play This Lesson in Very Slow Time

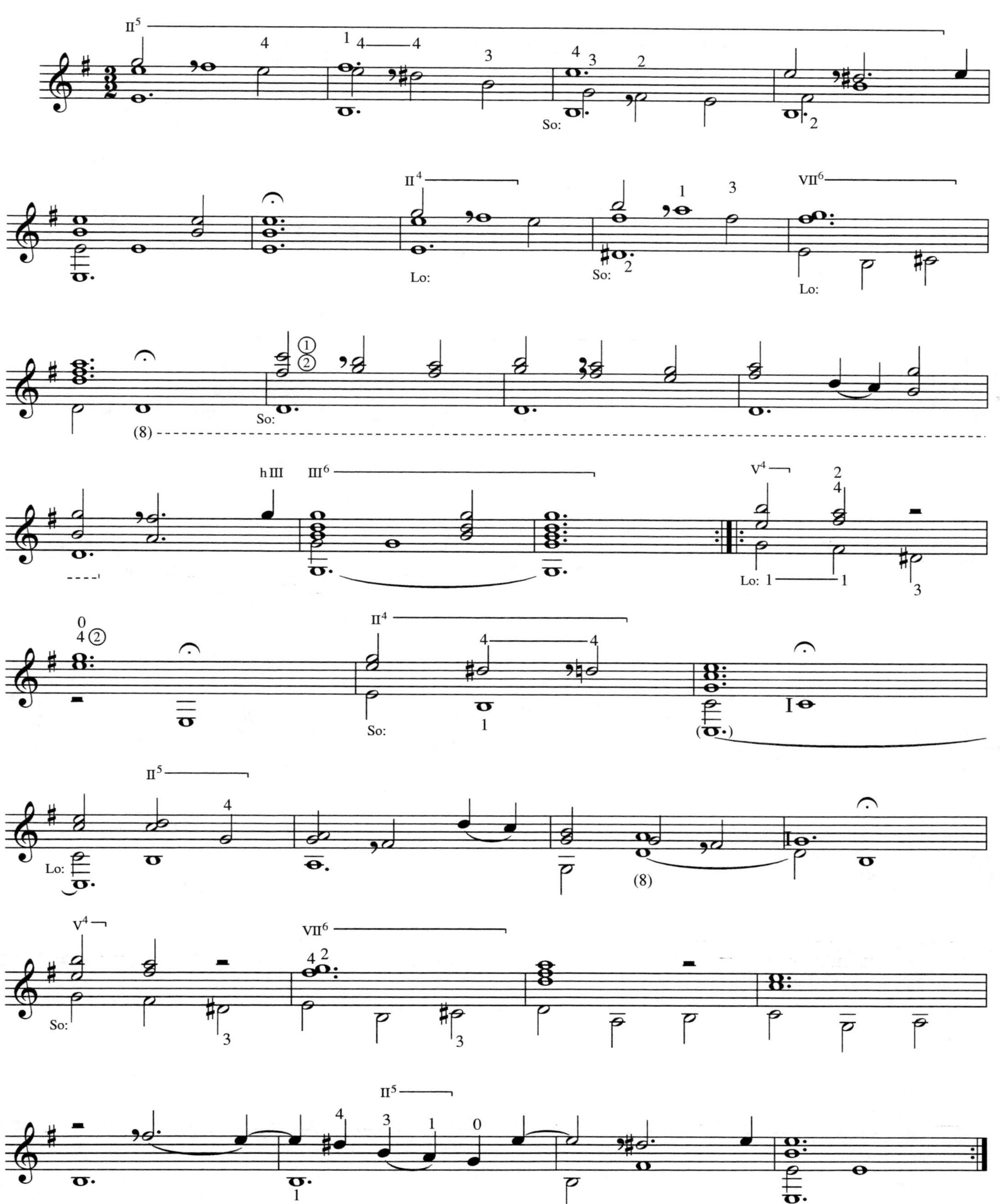

Seraband

II5
IX5
IX5
II5
h II
hIII
III6
II5

Suite No. 7

Transcribed and Edited by
Andrew Shepard-Smith

Thomas Mace
(c. 1612 - c. 1706)

Prælude

Allmaine I

(*) Mace indicates that to *crackle* a three-part stop is to "divide each stop with your thumb and two fingers, so as not to lose time - giving each crochet [quarter note] it's due quantity, adding prettiness by causing them to *sobb*." This is to be done by "slacking your left hand as soon as they are struck...just enough to suddenly deaden the sound."

Allmaine II
⑥=E
hII
So:
Lo:
Crackle
Coranto
Illegible one-beat anacrusis originally preceding measure 1
⑥=E
(*) Original bass note: e

(*) Original note: f♯

(**) Original note: b

Ringing or Bell Galliard

Original time signature: 12/4

⑥=E

Seraband

(*) Mace gives no direction on how to perform such a marking, however it is likely related to the *crackle*.

(**) Original bass note: d

Tattle de Moy

Suite No. 8

Transcribed and Edited by
Andrew Shepard-Smith

Thomas Mace
(c. 1612 - c. 1706)

(*) Illegible tablature note.

Allmaine

(*) Original note: d

Lo:
(8)
So:
VII⁵
II⁵
II³
V/VI⁵
VII⁶
Coranto
VI⁵
I

Seraband

Tattle de Moy

A Common Toy: Nightengal

(Derived from Chapter 40 of *Musick's Monument*)

Nightengal

Transcribed and Edited by
Andrew Shepard-Smith

Thomas Mace
(c. 1612 - c. 1706)

A Fancy Prælude or Voluntary

(Derived from Chapter 42 of *Musick's Monument*)

A Fancy Prælude or Voluntary
(originally G minor)
Transcribed and Edited by
Andrew Shepard-Smith
Thomas Mace
(c. 1612 - c. 1706)
⑥=E
So:
Lo:
(*) See end notes.

3
Lo:
So:
(8)
4
II5
VII5
5
So
III4
II4

Lo:
So:
I6
III4
(8)
6
(16)
VI6
III5
7

Lo:
So:
VII6
8
II5
II5
II5
(8)
(8)
V4
Lo:
So:
Lo:
Crackle
Crackle
(8)
Lo:
II5
II5
(8)
(8)
So:
9
(8)
Lo:
I6
Lo:

III⁴
So:
Lo:
(8)
Crackle
V³
10

(*) See end notes

Lo:
So:
cross-string
single-string

End Notes/ A Fancy Prelude or Voluntary

Mace states that, "Although this work seems long, the performer may leave off at any of the thirteen strains, indicated by the enclosed numbers at the double barlines."

Strain 1: The first two measures were originally one octave higher.

Strain 13: original fingerings, rhythms, and pitches

It seems unlikely that the lines placed after some of the bass notes in strain thirteen are used to indicate a spinger (see p. vii), although the markings appear identical. It is more probable that Mace used these lines to indicate that the duration of these bass notes should be at least an eighth note, or more likely a quarter note - a common indication in tablature.

Appendix

I. Biography

Thomas Mace (ca. 1612/13 - ca. 1706) is known primarily as an English composer, theorist, lutenist, luthier, vocalist, and violist. However, he is most known for authoring the theoretical treatise *Musick's Monument: or A Remembrancer of the Best Practical Musick* (1676).

Although his exact date of birth is not known, Mace must have been born in either 1612 or 1613, as he describes himself in a non-musical publication in 1698 as being eighty-six at the time of printing.[1] He was born in Cambridge, and the majority of his life was spent there, as he left on only a handful of occasions.[2]

Mace claims to have begun playing the lute in 1621, presumably at the age of nine. He states in *Musick's Monument,* "since this present year of 1675 – fifty-four years since I first began to undertake the instrument."[3] He must have had either a musical upbringing or a high aptitude in music, as he was, at about the age of twenty-three, appointed "singing-man" in 1635 at Trinity College, Cambridge under the direction of Robert Ramsey.[4] He later taught singing there and was associated with Trinity College until his final years.

It was also during this time (ca. 1635), as Mace states in *Musick's Monument,* that he was trying to marry his "most beloved, dearest, and sweetest living mistress" from Yorkshire.[5] After finally gaining her mother's consent, something at which he evidently spent considerable time on, the two wed in Yorkshire. Shortly thereafter, he returned to Cambridge. He fathered at least two children (likely two boys), as he mentions his "youngest son, John Mace," who took to the lute and viol at a young age, contrary to his expectations.[6]

When the English Civil War began in 1642, Mace's Royalist political views caused him to leave home.[7] And while he was a witness to the siege of York in 1644, he must have returned to Cambridge within at least a few years, as he is known to have given singing lessons there in 1647, although the War did not officially end until 1651. Clearly, he also survived the plague in Cambridge that occurred from 1665 to 1666.[8]

Nearing his middle sixties and having already started to write *Musick's Monument* in 1672, he took time in 1675 to write a tract concerning the condition of the highways in England (now in the British Museum) titled *The Profit, Conveniency, and Pleasure for the Whole Nation: being a short rational Discourse lately presented to his Majesty concerning the Highways of England: their badness, the causes thereof, the reasons of these causes, the impossibility of ever having them well mended according to the old way of mending: but may most certainly be done, and for ever so maintained (according to this NEW WAY) substantially and with very much ease, etc., etc. Printed for the public good in the year 1675.*[9] In this year, he also finished *Musick's Monument,* and is known to have journeyed to London to arrange for its publication.[10] He likely returned to Cambridge, only to travel back to London in 1690, where he stayed "for four months to sell instruments and music books which his increasing deafness made less useful to him."[11]

At the age of eighty-six, Mace's senescence and deafness did not bring an end to his authorship, as he wrote a booklet in 1698 titled *Riddles, Mervels and Rarities, or, A New Way of Health, from an Old Man's Experience,* where he celebrates that he is "healthful, lively, active and brisk" for an old man.[12] Published in his home town of Cambridge, this largely non-musical booklet contains only one musical example — a canon. Only eight years later, in 1706, Mace's *singing-man's* position at Trinity College is "voided by Mr. Mace."[13] Tilmouth and Spring suggest that, although other Maces were active in the choir, this could possibly suggest the death of Thomas Mace.[14] And although an exact date of death is uncertain, it could be asserted that this date either marked the end of his life, or he chose to resign his position at this time due to his age and severe deafness - living for perhaps several more years. Regardless, 1706 seems to mark at least the death of his musical life.

Mace left a lasting and *monumental* impression on English cathedral music, lute music, and viol music during his remarkably long life; his impact will no doubt survive for centuries more, educating scholars in the conservative style he represented. Aside from the music he presents in *Musick's Monument,* Mace is also known to have composed a verse-anthem, *I Heard a Voyce.*[15]

II. *Musick's Monument*

Musick's Monument, published in London in 1676, was written primarily between the years of 1672 and 1675, although it does contain music that was written as much as forty years earlier. In his treatise, Mace discusses four main topics which he has divided into three sections: parochial and cathedral music, the lute and theorboe, and the viol and music in general. The text as a whole contains much verse and is quite nostalgic, as Mace frequently recants times gone by. Tilmouth and Spring add that "Mace was a conservative. He believed that church music had reached perfection early in the century, and distrusted and disliked the extrovert qualities of the French style that began to find increasing favour at the Restoration and to oust more traditional forms of English instrumental music. *Musick's Monument*...is in fact a defense of the English tradition and an attempt to recover its values..."[16] Mace adds, in his Epistle to the Reader,

> "I write it not to please the itching vain of idle-headed fashionists, or gain their fond applause; I care for no such noise. I write it only for the sober sort, who love right musick, and will labour for't: and who will value worth in art, though old, and not affrighted with the good, though told 'tis out of fashion. By * – – of the nation (*the reader has liberty to put in what word he thinks most proper): I write it also, for to vindicate the * glory's instruments (*the lute), now out of date, and out of fashion grown, (as many tell) 'tis doubtful (sure) that all things are not well, when best things are most sleighted, though most rare. I write it likewise, for that fervent love I bear unto the lute, which far above most instruments I prize; this cannot be a fault; for all men have liberty, to like, and love, what they do most approve. I write it also, out of great good will unto my countreymen; and leave my skill behind me, for the sakes of those, that may not yet be born; but in some after-day may make good use of it, without abuse. But chiefly I do write it, for to show a duty to my maker, which I owe; and I no better way know how to do, than thus, to strive to make one tallent two: if thus too blame, I'le humbly bear my shame."[17]

Part one of *Musick's Monument* deals mainly with parochial (parish) and cathedral music. Although Mace emphatically declares that he is not Catholic, he was clearly a devoutly Christian man and his faith played a large role in the writing of this section as he covers such topics as how to properly sing psalms in church (with and without the aid of an organ), singing in tune, and the poor state of vocal music in the churches. His nostalgia, along with his conservatism, is evident through his belief that no music can be produced that is superior to the provisions already in place in the church, and he believes that "true musick [is] a certain divine-magical-spell, against all diabolical operations in the souls of men," and attempts, throughout the whole section, to guide the reader into the art of *true musick.*

Part two, titled "The Lute Made Easie," is the largest section of the book, containing forty-three chapters (including the music contained within this anthology). It is, in short, a method for learning all things having to do with the lute. In the first few chapters, he discusses the nature of the lute, along with accounts of the previous lute masters, including English lutenists J. Dowland and R. Johnson, and the Frenchman Gotiere (Gaultier). He answers common questions about the lute, discusses how to buy a lute (suggesting that those made by *Laux Maller* are the best), how to disassemble it, make repairs and mend cracks, re-string and re-fret it, and maintain it - basically, all things concerning the *mechanical* order of the lute.

After this discourse, he covers more performance related issues such as posture, proper use of the left and right hand, use of the fingertips versus the nails, and how to tune and read tablature. It is in this section that we see the *First and Second Sets of Præludes,* as he uses them as a pedagogical tool in guiding the beginning student into proper technique through the use of repertoire. He later introduces ornaments, or *graces* as he calls them, including a wonderful anecdote:

> "I, for my own part, have had occasion to break both my arms; by reason of which, I cannot make the *Nerve-Shake* well, nor strong; yet, by a certain motion of my arm, I have gain'd such a contentive *shake,* that sometimes my scholars will ask me how they shall do to get the like? I have then no better answer for them, than to tell them, they must first break their arm, as I have done; and so possibly, after that, (by practice) they may get my manner of shake."[18]

At this point, he introduces the lute suites and makes lengthy discussion about them, further defining each movement - including his own creation: the *Tattle de Moy.* And because Mace believes that there should be no discord in moving from one key to another, he includes many interludes (for each suite) to allow the performer to pass smoothly from one key to another.

The last section of *The Lute Made Easie* begins with a section on the *dyphone,* or the lute with fifty strings. Mace indicates that he invented and built this instrument in 1672 due to his *great defect in hearing,* claiming success by stating that it had a *"fuller, plumber, and lustier sound* than any other," no doubt due to the increased size and sympathetic vibrations.[19] The dyphone, as Mace states, is conveniently a combination of "the majestic theorboe, [for use] either for voice, organ, or consort, etc. and the high improved French lute, [to be used] for airy, and spruce, single or double lessons; and is also a most admirable consort instrument, where they know how to make the right use of it, and not suffer it to be over-top'd with squaling-scoulding-fiddles."[20] The theorboe half of the instrument bears twenty-six strings while the French lute holds twenty-four, where the treble strings of both are tuned to G-sol-re-ut. The head of the French lute is exactly the same as other French lutes, however the head of the theorboe, as he states, is much shorter. This was likely so that 1) it can be tuned more easily, 2) it is more proportionate (to which he claimed holding the dyphone was quite cumbersome), and 3) so that the shorter basses will not *over-ring* the trebles.[21] To this, he composed the following *rhime,* written in *Musick's Monument:*

I am of Old, and of Great Brittain's Fame,
 Theorboe was my Name
I'm not so Old; yet Grave, and much Accute,
 My Name was the French Lute.
But Since we are Thus Joyned Both in One,
 Henceforth Our name shall be The Lute Dyphone.
Loe Here a Perfect Emblem seen in Me,
 Of England, and of France, Their Unity:
Likewise That Year They did each other Aid,
 I was Contriv'd, and Thus Compleatly made
 Anno Dom. 1672
Long have we been Divided; now made One,
 We Sang in * 7th's,; Now in Full Unison.
In This Firm Unison, long may We Agree;
 No Unison's like that of Lute's Harmony.
Thus in It's Body, 'tis Trim, Spruce, and Fine;
 But in It's Sp'rit, 'tis like a Thing Divine.[22]

Immediately following his discourse on the dyphone, Mace concludes with a chapter concerning the theorboe. Here, he address the differences between it and the English lute, why it is necessary, and directions for tuning it and playing it. Ironically, Mace states that the theorboe is not to be used for solo work, as it is too large and ill-suited for such play, however, it is from this section that *A Fancy-Prælude or Voluntary* was taken, as it was composed for this instrument to be played as a solo. After this, Mace closes out *The Lute Made Easie* by explaining how theorbists are to read consort music.

All of the music within *The Lute Made Easie,* with the exception of the theorboe music, was written in tablature, and is to be played on a twelve-course lute, tuned appropriately for the particular suites. Tilmouth and Spring add that the "basic style ... is that of the Caroline period," and that "he aimed to draw together the best of this Anglo-French Style."[23] All of this can clearly be seen through his writings.

Part three of *Musick's Monument* is specifically a two-part treatise: on the viol, and on music in general. This section, containing only ten chapters, is about the same length as the first, however, Mace claims that it is more profitable than the lute section. He begins by discussing the faults in women's clothing fashion, followed by his musings on the poor quality of current music (believing the best music was that which he experienced in his youth). He then writes on the organ, the *harpsicon,* and a newly-invented English instrument, the pedal piano - which he believes excels all harpsicons and organs in solo and consort use. Next, he introduces his architectural plans for the design of the perfect *musick-room,* or auditorium for performance, complete with plans to include an organ and a pedal, a chimney, twelve galleries for auditors, four balconies, and arched ceilings.

This is followed by his plans for a *table organ* - an organ intended to serve the purpose of both a table and an organ. Mace believed such an instrument to be more suitable to consort music as it allows the performers to gather together in one place, around the organ, so that musical interaction can be much more intimate. One of the greatest benefits, however, is that this procedure gave the lute an opportunity to sound equally among the other consort instruments.

It is only in the fifth chapter that Mace even begins to discuss the viol; here he introduces posture, holding and using the bow, and tuning the viol. Tablature is included, complete with consort parts for the first piece – indicating that the following two works are to be played as solos. The last chapter concludes *Musick's Monument* and contains some of Mace's thoughts on music in general, including a spiral chart showing the relationship between music and God - again confirming his strong Christian ideals.

In conclusion, modern performers and scholars can find a great deal of wealth through the study of Mace's writings. His discourse on ornamentation and suite construction has long been identified as a strong source for scholars of performance practice. But it is ironic that his music, as contained in *Musick's Monument,* has yet to find a stronghold in modern concert halls - perhaps being overlooked by those in search of loftier suites by more well known composers within the academic canon, or possibly due to a lack of modern performance editions. There is no doubt, however, that Mace's music will eventually find its way into modern concert programs, as his music is, after more than three hundred years, still surprisingly fresh and infectiously melodic.

Endnotes:

[1] Michael Tilmouth and Matthew Spring, "Thomas Mace," *The New Grove Dictionary of Music and Musicians,* 2nd ed. Stanley Sadie (New York: Macmillan, 2001) 15: 465-67.

[2] The New Everyman Dictionary of Music. 6th ed. David Cummings (New York: Weidenfeld and Nicolson, 1988).

[3] Thomas Mace, *Musick's Monument,* facsimile reprint. Monuments of Music and Music Literature in Facsimile, Second Series, XVII (New York: Broude Brothers Limited, 1966): 39.

[4] *Choir of Trinity College, Cambridge.* August 2001 (London: Hyperion Records Limited, 2001) <http://www2.hyperion-records.co.records.co. uk/artist_page.asp?name=trinitychoir>.

[5] Mace, p. 122.

[6] Ibid., 45.

[7] Tilmouth and Spring, p. 465.

[8] Ibid.

[9] Samuel Smiles, *The Life of Thomas Telford.* August 2001 (Seattle, Washington: The World Wide School, 1997) <http://www.worldwideschool.org/library/books/hst/biography/The Life of Thomas Telford/chap2.html>.

[10] Tilmouth and Spring, p. 465.

[11] Ibid.

[12] Ibid.

[13] Ibid.

[14] Ibid.

[15] New Everyman Dictionary of Music.

[16] Tilmouth and Spring, p. 466.

[17] Mace, *Musick's Monument:* "A Short Epistle to the Reader..."

[18] Mace, p. 103.

[19] Ibid., p. 203.

[20] Ibid., p. 204.

[21] Ibid., p. 204-6.

[22] Ibid., p. 206.

[23] Tilmouth and Spring, p. 466

About the Author

Andrew Shepard-Smith, classical guitarist, is currently on staff at Vincennes University in Vincennes, Indiana. He has studied lute and guitar privately and in masterclasses with Renato Butturi, Clare Callahan, Eduardo Fernandez, Oscar Ghiglia, Michael Howell, Franco Platino, Paul Reilly, and Benjamin Verdery, among others. A scholar of early music, Shepard-Smith enjoys spending his time researching rather than practicing, transcribing rather than concertizing. His collections of transcription anthologies include composers such as Thomas Mace, Girolamo Frescobaldi, and the Spanish vihuelists. In addition, he is currently transcribing and editing the complete piano works of Enrique Granados for solo guitar. He resides in Vincennes, Indiana with his wife Vanessa and daughter Emily.

"Shepard-Smith's work shows a high-degree of scholarship and attention to detail in presenting for guitarists the lute music from Thomas Mace's historic Musick's Monument. *He has made a very valuable addition both to the performance repertoire and to the guitar reference literature."*

– Richard Yates –

"With this book we have a most important look into the mind of a Baroque master. The music is wonderful and the ornaments and text show the many possibilities of interpretation available to us today."

– Paul Reilly –

"Andrew Shepard-Smith's wonderful transcription/edition of Thomas Mace's music affords us a player's view of the 17th century fretboard and the musical mind animating its intriguing sounds. A valuable and welcome contribution!"

– Clare Callahan –

EXCELLENCE IN MUSIC
MEL BAY®
Since 1947